The
Traveler's
Psalm

The Traveler's Psalm

A 40-day Spiritual Journey

LOUISE R. CHAPMAN
MARY L. SCOTT
NINA G. GUNTER

Foreword by
Jerald D. Johnson

NAZARENE PUBLISHING HOUSE
Kansas City, Missouri

CONTENTS

NINA G. GUNTER

FOREWORD

When I learned that Louise Chapman, Mary Scott, and Nina Gunter collaborated to develop a book of devotional readings, my immediate response was—What a neat idea! These three ladies will always be remembered as special leaders of our church. They represent three generations, each one making a significant impact and giving us godly example over the years. While their expertise has been in the field of missions, their specialty has been to teach us to pray, give, and put God first in our lives.

Many of us have been influenced by Louise Robinson Chapman. As a missionary, as the wife of a general superintendent, and as general president of the denomination's missionary society, she carried out her roles with grace, dignity, and distinction. Who will ever forget her prayer of intercession at the 1989 General Assembly? Her special project of raising money for World Mission Radio prompted generous response from everywhere. What a lady!

There is also Mary Scott, whose own heroism and loyalty in the midst of difficult circumstances as a missionary prisoner of war has never ceased to inspire us. Her years of leadership as director of the Nazarene World Mission Society are marked by strong, assertive initiatives that served to keep the burden for reaching the lost on the denomination's front burner. During a portion of the time she served in this capacity, Mary and I were colleagues in administrative responsibilities, a period I'll always treasure in my memories.

And there is Nina Gunter—an example of how gifted and talented people who remain committed can continue what has been established by leaders of previous generations. As NWMS director, Nina is

God's servant who makes us aware of our responsibilities to take God's message to the whole world. It would appear that the mantle of Louise Robinson Chapman and of Mary Scott has fallen on Nina Gunter, and one must conclude that she is indeed worthy of such an honor.

Our church says "Thank you," ladies, for combining your spiritual insights to inspire us daily in our devotional reading.

—JERALD D. JOHNSON
General Superintendent

Louise R. Chapman

1. The Danger of the Tail Hold

I went out after [the lion], and smote him, and delivered [the lamb] out of his mouth: and when he arose against me, I caught him by his beard, and smote him, and slew him (1 Sam. 17:35, KJV).

The tail is the wrong part by which to grab hold. A newspaper article told of an elephant that broke loose from its owners and charged down the middle of a busy street in Mexico City. An onlooker, wishing to help corral the elephant, seized its tail when it plunged past. The beast turned, caught the tail-grabber in its huge trunk, and dashed him to the ground, killing him.

The beard is the proper place to fasten our hold if we expect to "rend apart" approaching lions. David, as a shepherd boy, caught a lion "by his beard" and slew it, thus delivering a terrified lamb. After the battle was over, David boasted in God, who delivered him "out of the paw of the lion."

Many of us fail to achieve victory because we take hold at the wrong place. When time is running out we make a desperate grab and get a tail hold, and then comes trouble and failure.

Some say a lion will not attack if you bravely look him in the eyes. I've never proved this with a real lion! David Livingstone once did, and it worked for him. I do know the technique works with spiritual lions.

We are in conflict. Now is the time to look our lions straight in the eyes, grab them by the beards, and rend them apart in the strength of the Lord.

I would be true, for there are those who trust me.
I would be pure, for there are those who care.
I would be strong, for there is much to suffer.
I would be brave, for there is much to dare.

—"I Would Be True"
Howard Arnold Walter
Sing to the Lord 493
Worship in Song 467

* * *

Father, grant unto me the daring faith with which David faced the lion and the caring faith with which Jesus faced the Cross. I am engaged in spiritual conflict with powerful forces. Your strength is my victory, for nothing can defeat those who trust in You. Amen.

2. Slippery Stones

Hold up my goings in thy paths, that my foot-steps slip not (Ps. 17:5, KJV).

While fishing for mountain trout in the Lewis River, I stepped on an innocent-looking stone, deceived by its green, mossy carpet. I slipped and tumbled into the cold, swift stream, throwing aside my rod, reel, and the silver trout I had already caught.

Unable to swim, I splashed over a waterfall, and the swift current tossed me to one side of the channel and then back into swirling depths. I grabbed for a big rock, clutching it with hands and feet. That stopped me just before I would have been swept around the bend into a whirlpool.

I looked about me. I was at the base of a huge rock in the midst of the rushing water, submerged to my neck. There I stayed until rescued by companions. Had it not been for kind friends and a loving God, I would never have come home alive.

I have been thinking lately of some slippery stones encountered in our spiritual journey.

One is carelessness in prayer life. Over this slippery stone millions have plunged to spiritual death. Nothing can ever take the place of prayer. People say they are too busy to pray. Many seem unable to prevail with God in prayer. From what I've seen and heard personally, I am convinced that the fires have gone out on thousands of Nazarene family altars. The stones have been removed, and only excuses remain.

Words can never measure the damage wrought by neglecting prayer. Examine your heart and hearth. If the fires have gone out, stones should be gathered and an altar erected this very day.

Another slippery rock is materialism. It crops out

in many forms. In the battles of this world a soldier does not want to be like his enemy. He does not want to wear the enemy's uniform. He does not want anyone to mistake him for the enemy. Are we slipping? Have we adopted the world's values?

The best way to keep from dying in a whirlpool is to keep off the slippery rocks.

> *His oath, His covenant, His blood,*
> *Support me in the whelming flood.*
> *When all around my soul gives way,*
> *He then is all my Hope and Stay.*
> *On Christ, the solid Rock, I stand;*
> *All other ground is sinking sand.*
>
> —"The Solid Rock"
> Edward Mote
> *Sing to the Lord* 436
> *Worship in Song* 92

* * *

Father in heaven, I am upon the earth where slippery places and treacherous currents abound. Guide my steps and keep me anchored to the Rock of Ages. My security is not in the strength of my grasp upon You but in the strength of Your grasp upon me. That is sufficient! Amen.

3. "Shoot to Kill!"

Then Elisha said, Shoot. And he shot (2 Kings 13:17, KJV).

A young seminary graduate was ready to begin his first pastorate. He had long observed and greatly admired Mrs. Booth Clibborn—a brave warrior who was then over 90 years of age. She could still pray the glory down, preach with tremendous power, and win scores of souls for her Lord.

The young preacher went to this daughter of General William Booth, saying, "For years I have observed your success as a Christian. I greatly admire your ability to accomplish things for the Lord. I aim to pattern my life after yours. I aim to pray like you pray. I aim to . . . I aim to . . . Could you give me a motto for the new life I am about to begin?"

Without a moment's hesitation the old warrior answered, with a shake of her finger, "Yes, young man, I can. Don't be forever aiming. Shoot! Shoot! Shoot to kill!"

Mere aiming accomplishes nothing. Too many are forever aiming to do what should be done, but they never shoot. They wait for a more convenient season to pull the trigger. When something should be done, the quickest and easiest way to do it is to take one good aim and then "shoot to kill!"

Rescue the perishing; Care for the dying;
   Snatch them in pity from sin and the grave.
Weep o'er the erring one; Lift up the fallen;
   Tell them of Jesus, the Mighty to Save.

—"Rescue the Perishing"
Fanny J. Crosby
Sing to the Lord 713
Worship in Song 349

* * *

Father, I serve the Christ who went about doing good, not merely aiming or planning to do good. I want to be like Him, forthright and zealous as a doer. I know that I should look before I leap, but I don't want to spend my life just looking. Help me to be as resolute in action as I am in intention. In His name. Amen.

4. It's Almost Sundown; Is Your Work Done?

Blessed is that servant, whom his lord when he cometh shall find so doing **(Matt. 24:46, KJV).**

On market Saturdays my parents journeyed to La Center, eight miles away, to swap our farm produce for supplies. When ready to leave they would promise, "We'll be back before sunset. Finish all your work, then play. If you're good, we will bring you some candy." We eight children, four boys and four girls, were each assigned tasks.

We were ordinary youngsters. We didn't mind the work and meant to obey, but only folks raised in large families can understand how much fun children can have when their parents are away for a whole day. As soon as the wagon disappeared over the hilltop, work ceased and play began.

"Shoot the Chutes" was our most daring sport. The huge barn roof served as an excellent chute. A high pile of straw on one side of the barn was our landing field. Anyone brave enough could sit on a slick plank or a sheet of tin and scoot from the peak of the barn to the straw pile. I can still feel the wind standing my hair on end as I sped down the barn roof.

We watered the cows at noon. Jersey milk cows are never supposed to be made excited. One of them, named Jessie, was especially nervous and would kick the milk pail and the milker when excited. On the Saturdays our parents were in town, we would open all the gates from the clover patch to the creek and play "Riding the Tails." The eight of us would yell like coyotes until the frightened herd ran full steam ahead. The older children would each catch a cow's tail, run till we fell, then hold on while the cows dragged us through the clover and into the woods. Jessie nearly always had her nervous breakdowns on Sunday mornings after our parents had been to the market on Saturdays.

Near sundown we would remember the promise of their return. Assigned work, barely begun, was instantly urgent. We knew what would happen if our parents found the tasks unfinished.

Suddenly the Robinson children became astonishingly industrious. We moved as if our lives, rather than our skins, depended upon completing the assignments. We willingly worked anywhere and everywhere, each overjoyed to do more than his or her share. The times we waited too late or our parents returned too early are indelibly printed on our memories.

Our Lord has promised His children, "I will come again." He gave us important work to do during His absence, and promised personal rewards to those who achieve it (Rev. 22:12).

The Christian Church has been somewhat like the Robinson children. We have been enjoying ourselves, "Shooting the Chutes" and "Riding the Tails." Now the sun is in the western sky, nearing the horizon. Much work remains undone. His impending return should motivate our accelerated pace.

> *Someday, when fades the golden sun*
> *Beneath the rosy-tinted west,*
> *My blessed Lord will say, "Well done!"*
> *And I shall enter into rest.*

—"Saved by Grace"
Fanny J. Crosby
Sing to the Lord 659
Worship in Song 260

* * *

Father, help me to "redeem the time," to "work while it is day." Let me not trifle away my opportunities, but so labor that I may greet the coming of Jesus with joy. How sad it would be to forfeit my reward! Keep me faithful, I pray. Amen.

5. Cries in the Night

Multitudes, multitudes in the valley of decision
(Joel 3:14, KJV).

"They cry in the night! They perish in the dark!" cried a dying pioneer missionary. Harmon Schmelzenbach, Sr., heard these words from a white rancher who lived on the high bank of the Limpopo River. Directly across the river on low-lying fertile land was a village of several hundred people. The white man and the Africans on the low bank were fast friends. The rancher owned a raft, his only means of crossing to visit the native village.

One night the crocodile-infested river suddenly rose seven or eight feet. Before villagers awoke to their danger the swollen waters had reached the huts on the outer rim of the village. Crocodiles snatched away sleeping children and some of the aged people lying near open fires. Piercing screams rent the darkness.

At ten o'clock the men were calling, "White man, come over and help us." The rancher told Schmelzenbach, "I wanted to help . . . I went to the edge of the waters and saw driftwood, floating huts, and dead animals carried by. I knew no living thing could cross that terrible torrent that night. I wrung my hands and tried to pray."

By eleven o'clock the whole village was shrieking, sobbing, moaning, and praying. By midnight the housetops, rocks, and trees were full of clinging dark forms. Their hoarse voices begged, "White man, help us!" A sudden scream, a splash, and one person after another fell or was pulled from his rock or tree. Frightened cries echoed from downriver as frail huts and fallen trees, borne by the swift current, carried

20

victims to certain death. Their final, desperate moans reached the ears of the tormented white man who paced the shore praying, "My God, why didn't I do what I knew I should have done!" Before two o'clock all was still.

For 6,000 years the river of life has been in flood. The Christian Church should have removed people from the island. While they pled poverty of resources and personnel the crocodiles of sin swallowed up millions of lost people. The night is upon us. The mad waters have cut off whole countries and nations. The people of these lands are crying, "Come and help us! We cannot survive here any longer."

How shall we remove the perishing from the clutches of this river of spiritual death? Thank God, we have a raft! God is the designer and builder of this raft. His Son is its pilot. On it we are crossing and recrossing. It looks frail, but it has proved its dependability in many a bitter storm. Its potential to accomplish the task has never been fully utilized. Let us go "all out for souls" to the uttermost parts of the earth!

Church of God, awaken; heed the Lord's command.
Tell the blessed story of the cross.
Fields are white for harvesting on ev'ry hand.
*Tell the blessed story of the cross.**

—"Tell the Blessed Story"
Haldor Lillenas
Sing to the Lord 695
Worship in Song 350

* * *

O Father, the noise of earth is one confused and desperate cry for help that only You can give and only the Church can channel. Grant to us hearing ears and caring hearts and reaching hands to save the lost from their threatened doom. Help me do what I can for them. In Jesus' name. Amen.

6. Do It Now

Give, and it shall be given unto you (Luke 6:38, KJV).

The pig asked the cow why people make so much fuss over cows and so little over pigs, since pigs are just as useful as cows. Said the pig, "They even use our feet, and yours are practically useless."

"The only thing I can figure out," said the cow, "is that you give only after you are dead, but we give all the time we are living."

"You can't sign any more checks one minute after you are dead." Better do it now.

"Do your own giving; don't leave it for other people to handle after you are gone."

> *Love ever gives,*
> *Forgives, outlives;*
> *And ever stands*
> *With open hands,*
> *For while it lives*
> *It gives.*
>
> —Selected

> *I gave My life for thee;*
> *   My precious blood I shed,*
> *That thou might'st ransomed be,*
> *   And quickened from the dead.*
> *I gave, I gave My life for thee.*
> *What hast thou giv'n for Me?*
>
> —"I Gave My Life for Thee"
> Frances R. Havergal
> *Sing to the Lord* 546
> *Worship in Song* 284

* * *

Gracious Father, You gave Your only Son, and He gave His very life, that I might know and serve You. I cannot match so great a love and sacrifice, but let my giving at least reflect the spirit of Calvary! Amen.

7. Collective Power

We are labourers together with God (1 Cor. 3:9, KJV).

When E. E. Hale visited Switzerland he was greatly impressed to find that almost every Swiss home was a small watch or clock factory. Each house had a corner or shop where some part of these timepieces was being manufactured. All of the men, women, and children proudly worked together to make the whole of Switzerland the world's clock and watch shop.

The task of evangelizing the world is both an individual and a collective challenge and responsibility. The importance of the individual cannot be overstressed. I am debtor. I am responsible. I can be a point of beginning from which God puts mighty forces into action. I have a work that no other can do. Therefore I must be faithful. I must not fail Him in even one of the lesser requirements.

It took all the homes of all the people to make Switzerland the world's clock and watch shop. Oh, that God might have all the homes and all the people of all the churches joined together in exalting Christ that He might be seen by all mankind. Alone, no person can go into all the world, but together we can reach the uttermost parts. United participation accumulates tremendous potential.

As great as the world's need, so great should be our power. No world crisis or threatening storm will ever change God's love or lessen His power. He is trying today to instill in us a greater sense of urgency than we have ever felt before. Will we cooperate?

Like a mighty army Moves the Church of God.
Christians, we are treading Where the saints have trod.
We are not divided; All one body we:
One in hope and doctrine, One in charity.

—"Onward, Christian Soldiers"
Sabine Baring-Gould
Sing to the Lord 644
Worship in Song 319

* * *

Holy Father, the mission of the Church exceeds the assets and abilities of any one person or group. We are all needed to complete this awesome task. Help me to add my portion of wealth and work to the mission, engaged with others and with You in an assignment that has eternal consequences. Amen.

8. The Big Difference

Freely ye have received, freely give **(Matt. 10:8, KJV).**

Many of us sleep in heated houses under electric blankets. In some parts of the world several children cling together under one worn goatskin, or huddle in piercing cold like little animals underneath elevated huts. Thousands stretch out on cold streets or roadways, having no houses or beds.

We enjoy beefsteak in a paradise of plenty. We eat an average of 72 percent above the standard body requirement. Over half the world will lie down in hunger tonight.

We can rely on doctors, nurses, hospitals, inoculations, and vitamins. In many places the people have only witch doctors, evil spirits, and superstitious fears. Millions suffer needless physical and mental torture. Multitudes die prematurely.

We indulge and pamper our children, driving them to church and school, giving them spending money, and shielding them from work. In many places homeless waifs feed from garbage cans, sleep in boxes, cover themselves with rags, and wander about unwanted, untended, and diseased.

Many of us have known nothing but freedom. We speak and print our likes, dislikes, and complaints. Millions enjoy no freedom of speech, travel, or religion. No wonder some nations feel that the scales of justice are unbalanced!

What has brought about this big difference? We have had the gospel of Jesus Christ! Christ is the only sufficient answer to the world's need. Always this has been, is now, and ever shall be. It is Christ or chaos.

In our meditation, let us stand in the shoes of our

spiritually and temporally deprived brothers and sisters. Then let us give in love, prayer, service, and money just as we would want them to do if the scales were unbalanced in their favor.

> *He spent His life in doing good;*
> *I want to be like Jesus.*
> *In lowly paths of service trod;*
> *I want to be like Jesus.*
> *He sympathized with hearts distressed,*
> *He spoke the words that cheered and blessed,*
> *He welcomed sinners to His breast.*
> *I want to be like Jesus.**

—"I Want to Be Like Jesus"
Thomas O. Chisholm
Sing to the Lord 208
Worship in Song 40

* * *

Deliver me, O loving Father, from self-indulgence. Keep me from thinking that all that is given to me is given for me. Much of it is meant for others whose needs are greater than mine. Help me to care and to share in the spirit of Jesus. I pray this in His name. Amen!

---

9. The Loyal Eleven

Then the eleven disciples went away into Galilee, into a mountain where Jesus had appointed them (Matt. 28:16, KJV).

All around the world I find Nazarenes sacrificing, giving, working, and pushing forward for God and holiness.

Why is it so easy to forget the many good folks who try hard to please God and to extend His kingdom while a few cantankerous ones, like sore thumbs, get most of the attention?

True, there are always some who are not what Christians should be. Some will be shallow, or money grabbers, or careless, self-centered, and worldly. Some may be downright sinners.

The church, like every other group, has always had problems and problem people. It always will have. If we look too long and too closely at this class, our lives could become bitter and critical. It is even possible for one's spirit to become more unchristlike than the thing he condemns.

Twelve men followed Jesus. Twelve men sat at His feet. One of the 12 was Judas. The Early Christian Church kept their eyes upon the 11, not on the lone betrayer. See what the 11 did! All we value and enjoy today in the spiritual realm has resulted from the faithfulness of those 11 disciples.

We do have problems. While we handle the problems and confess our needs, let us keep our eyes upon Christ and the great group who so wholeheartedly love and serve Him.

For all the saints who from their labors rest,
Who Thee by faith before the world confessed,
Thy name, O Jesus, be forever blest.
Alleluia! Alleluia!

—"For All the Saints"
William W. How
Sing to the Lord 685
Worship in Song 310

* * *

Almighty Father, thank You for all who have served and are serving You faithfully. They encourage my heart and inspire my faith. Keep their examples before me, and let me not be soured or scared by those who have betrayed and forsaken Christ. Amen.

10. Power to Bring Forth

The children are come to the birth, and there is not strength to bring forth (**Isa. 37:3, KJV**).

God has blessed the Church of the Nazarene. He has given us noble leadership. Our people are unexcelled. Our message is the needed message. Our organizations, our methods, and our programs are sufficient.

In this day of world crises the Church of the Nazarene should play a leading role. We try hard. We grind early and late. Everywhere we face the fact that "there is not strength to bring forth." Our insufficiency reminds me of a hand mill on which we ground our corn in the early days in Swaziland.

It was a good hand mill. It gave more and better meal than we had when we ground our corn on stones, but the output was hopelessly inadequate. It took all our strength and 18 hours of grinding daily to barely keep our mission supplied.

One day we bought a gasoline engine. We harnessed it to the mill with strong leather bands. When the engine began to turn, the mill poured out sack after sack of fine, white meal. In a short time, there was more meal than we could use for ourselves and our neighbors.

Why not stop our hand grinding and harness our machinery to Omnipotence with bands of intercessory prayer? Then we can grind grist for ourselves, our neighbors, and the entire hungry world.

"As soon as Zion travailed, she brought forth" (Isa. 66:8, KJV).

Lord, send the old-time power, the Pentecostal power!
Thy floodgates of blessing on us throw open wide!
Lord, send the old-time power, the Pentecostal power,
That sinners be converted and Thy name glorified!

—"Pentecostal Power"
Charlotte G. Homer
Sing to the Lord 290
Worship in Song 273

*   *   *

Father, I am weak but You are strong. You give power to the faint. Help me to claim that promise in prayer and by faith. In Your gift of strength I can prevail over all opposing forces and over all personal inadequacies. Then I can report to You with joy, "Mission accomplished."

11. Raising Our Own Kittens

Train up a child in the way he should go: and when he is old, he will not depart from it (Prov. 22:6, KJV).

Dr. Chapman told of an old miller who didn't want to be troubled with kittens, so he did away with all the cats. Soon the rats took over the mill, tearing open his sacks and devouring his meal.

To destroy the rats he needed cats, so he gathered all kinds of big cats from the neighborhood. He put them in the mill and fed and petted them to make them feel at home.

When he returned to his milling the wheels squeaked and the cogs pounded with a fearful and deafening sound. Every cat stopped lapping milk. With backs humped and tails erect they shot out of the open doors and windows and were seen no more.

The old miller learned his lesson. Since he must have cats, he would raise his own kittens. When his mill squeaked and the wheels ground, the kittens who were raised with those noises would merely think, "This sounds like home."

If tomorrow we want to have preachers and missionaries, if we want laypersons to support the mission of the Church, if we want folks who will stay with us when the grist grinds noisily, we must raise our own kittens in our own mill today.

Our boys and girls are the most important part of the Church. I have seen children participating efficiently in the church services. I have heard them pray intelligently and definitely for shared requests. I am convinced that children can do anything adults do in our service to the Lord. Check up on the kittens.

O give us homes built firm upon the Savior,
  Where Christ is Head and Counselor and Guide;
Where ev'ry child is taught His love and favor
  *And gives his heart to Christ, the Crucified.**

—"A Christian Home"
Barbara B. Hart
Sing to the Lord 727
Worship in Song 499

*   *   *

Heavenly Father, may our children, like Timothy, know from earliest years "the holy scriptures," which can make them "wise unto salvation through faith . . . in Christ Jesus." Help us to teach them well, both in words and deeds. In His name. Amen.

---

12. Beat a Charge

Speak unto the children of Israel, that they go forward (Exod. 14:15, KJV).

A vastly outnumbered and desperately struggling little army was almost surrounded by its foe. There seemed but one strategy left. The commander shouted to the drummer boy, "Beat a retreat!"

The drum beat faster and louder.

The officer ran to the drummer. "I said beat a retreat," he roared. "It will soon be too late."

"I was never taught to beat a retreat," the frightened lad replied. Sensing the desperation of his beloved commander, he cried, "But, Sir, I do know how to beat a charge. I can beat a charge that will cause dead men to stand on their feet."

"Then beat a charge," the harassed officer ordered. At the startling call of the exploding drum, the fainting soldiers leaped forward. Facing the unexpected onrush of the charging army, the foe broke ranks and fled. A great military victory was won because a bravehearted drummer boy did not know how to beat a retreat.

Our Lord never taught us how to beat a retreat. With Him it is always, "Forward!" We are in the midst of a mighty conflict. Battle and death are on every side. Do you feel outnumbered? Weak? Beat a charge! Beat a charge!

God can help you beat a charge that will rouse the very dead to action. Ask God to help you beat that charge. There are too many who have never tried to do anything really magnificent for Him!

Rouse then, soldiers; rally round the banner.
Ready, steady, pass the word along.
Onward, forward, shout aloud "Hosanna!"
Christ is Captain of the mighty throng.

—"Sound the Battle Cry"
William F. Sherwin
Sing to the Lord 647
Worship in Song 324

*　*　*

Lord of hosts, our trust is in You. At Your command we will "fight the good fight of faith" and "lay hold on eternal life." Our cause is worth fighting for. Our Christ is worth living and dying for. We have enlisted for the duration, and our one direction is forward. May I prove "a good soldier of Jesus Christ" at my point in the battle line. Amen.

Mary L. Scott

13. A Prescription for Everyday Living

Be joyful always; pray continually; give thanks in all circumstances, for this is God's will for you in Christ Jesus (1 Thess. 5:16-18).

God's will for us includes daily life, not just "big things" like choosing a companion, a vocation, or our next move. In this scripture Paul mentions three ingredients in the will of God for our whole lives.

1. "Be joyful always." We are prone to emphasize the tragic and negative. We should dwell on our faith instead. Phillips translates, "Be happy in your faith at all times." Be happy in God's love and care.

We cannot choose what enters our lives, but we can choose the attitudes we take. Resentment ends in bitterness; resignation is pagan. We can fix our attention on the dark side, or we can seek to learn what God is trying to teach us, not forgetting to look at the many blessings and mercies He has bestowed. Rejoicing brings victory and fulfills God's will for us.

Dr. Culbertson, in *More like the Master*, says that you should look at every problem you face in yourself, in your relations with others, or in your circumstances as, first, an opportunity to grow in grace; second, as an opportunity for God to show His power.*

---

*Paul T. Culbertson, *More Like the Master* (Kansas City: Beacon Hill Press of Kansas City, 1966), 116.

2. "Pray continually." Goodspeed translates this phrase, "Never give up praying." Praying is not begging or demanding for personal benefit or pleasure. Real prayer is for the will of God to be done. Pray until God changes things, people, and you. Pray until God meets you in assurance and speaks to you.

Dr. A. F. Harper told of a young flyer who was making his first solo flight. He checked the plane carefully and took off. Soon he noticed a strange sound. Looking around he discovered a rat gnawing at a vital part of the plane.

It was before the days of automatic controls, so he could not leave the pilot's seat to chase away the rat. Suddenly he remembered a statement from his training: "Rats can't live in high altitudes." He climbed to a higher altitude and the noise decreased and then stopped. The rat was dead.

There are many annoying, gnawing circumstances in life that we cannot change, but we can set the levers of our souls to rise through prayer to the very presence of God.

3. "Give thanks in all circumstances." Various translations of this are illuminating. Phillips renders it, "Be thankful, whatever the circumstances may be." Goodspeed says, "Thank God whatever happens." Paul, in Eph. 5:20, exhorts us to "always [give] thanks to God the Father for everything, in the name of our Lord Jesus Christ."

How can we do this? Because we have faith in God. He knows what is best for us. Nothing can enter our lives apart from His permissive will. We do not always understand, but we can trust Him. "And we know that in all things God works for the good of those who love him, who have been called according to his purpose" (Rom. 8:28).

Be still, my soul; the Lord is on thy side.
  Bear patiently the cross of grief or pain.
Leave to thy God to order and provide;
  In ev'ry change He faithful will remain.
Be still, my soul; thy best, thy heav'nly Friend
Thro' thorny ways leads to a joyful end.

—"Be Still, My Soul"
Katharina von Schlegel
Sing to the Lord 97
Worship in Song 41

* * *

Heavenly Father, You clothe the lilies and feed the sparrows, yet lilies die and sparrows fall. Life brings to all both good and bad, both joy and sorrow. Through it all I choose to trust Your love, wisdom, and power. I will rejoice and give praise in Jesus' name. Amen.

14. Faithful

He who is faithful in what is least is faithful also in much **(Luke 16:10, NKJV).**

It is only natural to want to succeed at whatever we do. It is also natural to want to engage in work that brings results, especially when serving the Lord. In spiritual warfare—seeking to proclaim the good news of salvation to all people, at home and abroad—we need frontline troops such as missionaries, national preachers, and committed laypersons. But this spiritual warfare demands the total participation of us all, not just the frontline troops. No country succeeds in war by the power of its military alone. Even the great Napoleon was defeated when his supply lines failed.

A layman came to me after a service and said, "You missionaries will receive a great reward." I don't believe any missionary will receive a greater reward than the least-known, unpraised layperson or pastor who has been faithful in the tasks God has given them. God is interested less in our abilities than in our availability. Can He have all of you?

The reward is not to the brilliant, the spectacular, or even to the successful. The reward is to the faithful. In the parable of the talents the lord of the servants said to the one who had gained five more talents, "Well done, good and faithful servant; you were faithful over a few things, I will make you ruler over many things. Enter into the joy of your lord" (Matt. 25:21, NKJV).

All of us can be as good as the grace of God can make us; and all of us can be faithful.

I am resolved to follow the Savior,
    Faithful and true each day,
Heed what He sayeth, do what He willeth;
    He is the Living Way.

—"I Am Resolved"
Palmer Hartsough
Sing to the Lord 487
Worship in Song 372

*   *   *

How great is Your faithfulness, my Father! Enable me to be faithful, also, as the servant of Your will, wherever You send, whatever it costs. I do not pray to be successful or esteemed in the eyes of the world, but I do pray to be successful in Your eyes. To hear Your "well done" is the deepest desire of my heart. Amen.

15. Treasures in Clay Jars

For God, who said, "Let light shine out of darkness," made his light shine in our hearts to give us the light of the knowledge of the glory of God in the face of Christ. But we have this treasure in jars of clay to show that this all-surpassing power is from God and not from us (2 Cor. 4:6-7).

God, who brought the light of life into our world, has shined gospel light into our hearts with power to save from sin.

What did Paul mean when he said we have this treasure in jars of clay? Those to whom he wrote understood clearly. Since there were no insured banks in which to deposit their wealth, clay jars were often used to store their life's savings. The jars were buried near their homes. They also used clay jars to store grain, cloth, food, water, and wine. The Dead Sea scrolls were preserved in clay jars for nearly 2,000 years. Just so, the glorious light of the gospel is deposited in our human hearts.

The purpose of such common receptacles is to show that "this all-surpassing power is from God and not from us." The weakness of man serves to magnify the power of God. The good that is done is so evidently by the power of God that no one can share the glory with Him.

The jars of clay are subject to stress but not to destruction. Paul affirms this in figures borrowed from the Corinthian games held each fifth year:

hard pressed—but not crushed
perplexed—but not in despair
persecuted—but not abandoned
struck down—but not destroyed

In all these circumstances the life of Jesus is revealed in our mortal bodies.

> *Strong are the foes that conquer I must.*
> *Long is the way, but in Thee I trust.*
> *In my own strength but weakness I see.*
> *Grant me a closer walk with Thee.*[*]

—"A Closer Walk with Thee"
Haldor Lillenas
Sing to the Lord 617
Worship in Song 38

*   *   *

Almighty Father, for the sake of the treasure within, preserve the earthen vessel through another day. I pray not that the vessel be spared from trouble but that the treasure be shared with joy. I gladly concede to You all the glory, honor, and praise. Amen.

16. Self or Others?

Likewise the chief priests also, together with the scribes, mocked and said among themselves, "He saved others; Himself He cannot save" **(Mark 15:31, NKJV).**

This was the testimony of His persecutors and enemies as Jesus hung on the Cross. How true their first statement was: "He saved others." During His three years of public ministry He saved lepers from disease and ostracism; He saved a widow's only son from death; He saved a Syro-Phoenician woman from demons and a paralytic from his sins.

But His accusers were mistaken when they said He could not save himself. At His request the Father would have dispatched a host of angels to rescue Him from His crucifiers (Matt. 26:53). His enemies had power over Him only by the Father's permission (John 19:10-11).

Had Jesus saved himself He could not have saved us. He would have disqualified himself as the Savior of the world. The taunt of His enemies expressed a fundamental principle of His life and death and of our true discipleship.

What about us who follow Him? We are the bridge between people lost in sin and Jesus the Savior. Are we saving ourselves or investing our time to pray for the lost, our abilities to bring the lost to Him, our resources and treasure in Kingdom business?

His Spirit fill my hung'ring soul,
His power all my life control.
My deepest prayer, my highest goal—
*That I may be like Jesus.**

—"I Want to Be Like Jesus"
Thomas O. Chisholm
Sing to the Lord 208
Worship in Song 40

* * *

Father, help me to not spare myself but to invest myself. Like Paul, help me to spend and to be spent for others. Like Jesus Christ, help me to prefer death in service to life in self-indulgence. Only Your grace can furnish me with the needed love and courage. Let that grace abound toward me. Amen.

17. The Traveler's Psalm

Behold, He who keeps Israel shall neither slumber nor sleep (Ps. 121:4, NKJV).

Psalm 121 is commonly known as the traveler's psalm. It was one of the songs of ascent sung by Jewish pilgrims as they made their way to Jerusalem. It expresses the safety they felt under the watchful eye of God.

This psalm became real to three new China missionaries at Christmastime in 1940. A Mennonite couple and I decided to visit our respective mission stations during language school break. The stations were in territory occupied by the Japanese. When our travel passes were granted we informed our missionaries of the scheduled arrival time at Hantan, the nearest railroad station to our compounds at Taming.

No one was there to meet us. We went to an inn to await daylight and learned that no bus would depart for Taming until the next day. Since it was cold we rented a room with a "stove," which was an oil drum with no chimney. We put on all the clothing we had and retired early, anticipating a good night's sleep.

About ten o'clock I was awakened with an urgent impression to get up. I lay there shivering for a few minutes and the Voice (not audible but real) came again: "You'd better get up." I decided to get up and go to the "stove" to get warm. As I neared the missionary couple's bed my knees buckled and I said, "I feel faint." The Mennonite woman was a nurse and sensed the danger immediately. She flung the door wide to let fresh air in.

I am confident that God sent His guardian angel to awaken "green" missionaries who had closed the door tightly, allowing carbon dioxide from an un-vented "stove" to fill the room. We were within min-utes of sleeping into eternity, but "He who keeps Israel shall neither slumber nor sleep." By morning we were almost completely recovered from the illness caused by the poisonous air, and we completed our visit with joy.

When I travel the pathway so rugged and steep,
When I pass thro' the valley so dark and so deep,
And when snares for my soul by my foes have been set,
Jesus never has failed me yet.

—"He Never Has Failed Me Yet"
W. J. Henry
Sing to the Lord 565
Worship in Song 443

* * *

O watchful Father, I commit to You the entire journey of life. Nothing surprises Your wisdom, nothing ex-hausts Your power, nothing quenches Your love. You are truly the refuge and defense of Your people in every situation of trial or trouble. Keep me, in Jesus' name. Amen.

18. Light for Darkness

This is the message we have heard from him and proclaim to you, that God is light and in him there is no darkness at all (1 John 1:5, NRSV). The light shines in the darkness, and the darkness did not overcome it (John 1:5, NRSV).

Light implies darkness. Many factors contribute to the darkness of our times. As far as man is concerned the battle began in the garden of Eden, when the first man heeded the powers of darkness and disobeyed the will of God. This rebellion brought darkness to all mankind, and it persists to the present day.

Darkness abounds in many concrete forms: crime, the spirit of rebellion and anarchy, the breakdown in morals and common decency, premarital sex, college "shack ups," homosexuality, alcohol and drug abuse, and the breakdown in integrity and honesty resulting in widespread corruption in government, business, and private lives.

Yes, there is darkness. But, thank God, there is light. Light dispels darkness, however small the light, however dense the darkness. God is light. Jesus said, "I am the light of the world." He is One who cleansed the lepers, healed the sick, delivered from demons, raised the dead, died on the Cross, but rose triumphantly and is alive forever! "Therefore he is able to save completely those who come to God through him, because he always lives to intercede for them" (Heb. 7:25).

Jesus also said, "You are the light of the world. . . . let your light shine before men, that they may see your good deeds and praise your Father in heaven" (Matt. 5:14, 16). Our task in this dark world is to lift up Christ as His light shines through us.

Cursing the darkness never saves anyone. Lighting the pathway does.

> *There's a call comes ringing o'er the restless wave:*
>   *"Send the light! Send the light!"*
> *There are souls to rescue, there are souls to save,*
>   *Send the light! Send the light!*

—"Send the Light"
Charles H. Gabriel
Sing to the Lord 705
Worship in Song 351

*   *   *

How great is the darkness, Heavenly Father, but how much greater is the light! My life is such a small light, yet even gross darkness cannot overcome those who shine for You. Use me today to help someone escape the sunless prison of sin and discover Jesus, who is "the light of the world." I pray this in His name and for Your glory. Amen.

19. The Spirit-filled Life: Trouble

Be filled with the Spirit (Eph. 5:18).

God wills that each of us live a Spirit-filled life. The provision for such a life is plainly taught in the Scriptures: "I will pour out my Spirit on all people. Your sons and daughters will prophesy, your old men will dream dreams, your young men will see visions" (Joel 2:28). Jesus also promised, "I will ask the Father, and he will give you another Counselor to be with you forever—the Spirit of truth" (John 14:16-17).

Some years ago H. K. Bedwell, a Nazarene missionary in Africa, wrote a series of articles on false ideas of the Spirit-filled life. He pointed out that some people insist that the Spirit-filled life brings exemption from trouble. But Jesus clearly told His disciples, "In this world you will have trouble. But take heart! I have overcome the world" (John 16:33).

The fact is, the Spirit-filled life means victory and preservation in the midst of trouble. The three Hebrew young men were not saved from being thrown into the fiery furnace, but God went with them into the flames and brought them out victorious. It is worth having trouble to experience the comfort and deliverance God brings. Spurgeon once said, "There are no crown wearers in heaven who were not cross bearers on earth."

The consecrated cross I'll bear
Till death shall set me free;
And then go home my crown to wear,
For there's a crown for me.

—"Must Jesus Bear the Cross Alone?"
Thomas Shepherd
Sing to the Lord 547
Worship in Song 146

* * *

Righteous Father, I do not ask You for an easier way. Rather, I ask You for a deeper love, a greater faith, and a stronger hope. When I think of Jesus, and the martyrs who confessed Him so gallantly and expensively, I would be ashamed to dodge the cross and appease the world. Enable me to be triumphant in trouble. Amen.

20. The Spirit-filled Life: Temptation

Because he himself suffered when he was tempted, he is able to help those who are being tempted (Heb. 2:18).

Some say that when the sin principle has been cleansed from the heart there can be no temptation to evil. We have only to look at the facts to realize that this is a false conception. Adam was created without sin, yet he was tempted as he yielded. Jesus, the "last Adam," had no sin in His heart, yet the Bible tells us that He was tempted by Satan.

In the Spirit-filled life we are enabled to triumph over temptation. Temptation is not sin. Some over-conscientious Christians think the devil's accusations and temptations are convictions from the Spirit. A common human illustration may help here. Proposal is not marriage. The proposal can be rejected just as the proposal to do or think evil can be rejected. The chief danger in temptation is entering into discussion or conference with the enemy of our souls. We must learn to say a final and definite no to the devil.

Jesus told His disciples in the garden of Gethsemane to "watch and pray so that you will not fall into temptation" (Matt. 26:41). Watchfulness and prayer will help us to recognize the wiles of the enemy. "No temptation has seized you except what is common to man. And God is faithful; he will not let you be tempted beyond what you can bear. But when you are tempted, he will also provide a way out so that you can stand up under it" (1 Cor. 10:13).

Yield not to temptation,
For yielding is sin.
Each vict'ry will help you
Some other to win.

—"Yield Not to Temptation"
Horatio R. Palmer
Sing to the Lord 638
Worship in Song 436

* * *

Holy Father, You cannot be tempted, but I cannot escape being tempted. Give me grace to overcome the tempter as I trust in the Savior, who was himself tempted but triumphant. I know that He emerged with victory through knowledge and application of the Scriptures. Teach me Your word and give me Your wisdom, I humbly ask in His name. Amen.

21. The Spirit-filled Life: Emotion

In this you greatly rejoice, though now for a little while you may have had to suffer grief in all kinds of trials. These have come so that your faith—of greater worth than gold, which perishes even though refined by fire—may be proved genuine and may result in praise, glory and honor when Jesus Christ is revealed (1 Pet. 1:6-7).

Emotions are governed by many factors, including physical condition, environment, circumstances, and "heaviness through manifold temptation." Some have thought that in the Spirit-filled life one will always feel happy. But Peter encourages his readers by exhorting them to rejoice in their faith in the midst of suffering. God gives peace and joy that pass understanding.

The disciples rejoiced even when flogged. "The apostles left the Sanhedrin, rejoicing because they had been counted worthy of suffering disgrace for the Name" (Acts 5:41). Genuine faith remains steady though feelings change. Jesus did not feel happy when He wept over Jerusalem, or when He declared, "My soul is overwhelmed with sorrow to the point of death" (Matt. 26:38).

Madame Guyon said, "It is a great truth, wonderful as it is undeniable, that all our happiness, temporal, spiritual, and eternal, consists in this one thing: namely in resigning ourselves to God, and leaving ourselves with Him to do with us and in us just as He pleases."

There are times when we are swept along on currents of joy. Service is easy; prayer is a delight. But there also come seasons of dryness and heaviness. These can be periods of great growth, however, when we go forward, not by feelings but by faith and fixed purpose.

> *Help me then, in ev'ry tribulation,*
> *So to trust Thy promises, O Lord,*
> *That I lose not faith's sweet consolation,*
> *Offered me within Thy holy Word.*
> *Help me, Lord, when toil and trouble meeting,*
> *E'er to take, as from a Father's hand,*
> *One by one, the days, the moments fleeting,*
> *Till I reach the promised land.*

> —"Day by Day"
> Caroline V. Sandell-Berg
> *Sing to the Lord* 105
> *Worship in Song* 61

* * *

Father, I trust in You, not in my feelings. Your love is unchanging, my feelings are fickle. Leaning upon You, I cannot fall. Depending upon my feelings, I cannot stand. Uphold me and inspirit me for this day's trials and toils, I pray in Jesus' name. Amen.

22. The Spirit-filled Life: Discipline

God disciplines us for our good, that we may share in his holiness (Heb. 12:10).

It is dangerously false to suppose that if we are filled with the Spirit discipline becomes unnecessary. Discipline means to subject ourselves to control—God's control. "The fruit of the Spirit" includes "self-control" (Gal. 5:22-23). When we totally surrender our wills to God, He reappoints them as His representatives in controlling the mind, body, and spirit.

In 2 Cor. 10:5 Paul says, "We demolish arguments and every pretension that sets itself up against the knowledge of God, and we take captive every thought to make it obedient to Christ." In Paul's day Greek philosophy and ethics were greatly respected and practiced. But Paul said all these must be judged by the principles of Christ. He exhorts us to throw out all thoughts unworthy of Christ. We cannot prevent the devil from making evil suggestions, but we can refuse to entertain them. Paul gives the best protection for the mind: "Finally, brothers, whatever is true, whatever is noble, whatever is right, whatever is pure, whatever is lovely, whatever is admirable—if anything is excellent or praiseworthy—think about such things" (Phil. 4:8).

Not only is discipline needed to control the mind, but it is essential for controling the body—even the normal natural drives. Joseph demonstrated this discipline in refusing to commit adultery with Potiphar's wife. Samson lost his freedom, sight, and strength because he could not say no to his bodily appetites. Paul cites his own wise example when exhorting the Corinthians: "But I discipline my body and bring it into subjection, lest, when I have preached to others, I myself should become disqualified" (1 Cor. 9:27, NKJV).

The Psalmist, well aware of the necessity of controlling the tongue and speech, wrote, "Set a guard, O Lord, over my mouth; keep watch over the door of my lips" (Ps. 141:3, NKJV). Gossip has slain many characters. We are familiar with the three tests before repeating tales: Is it true? Is it kind? Is it necessary? If we apply these principles, most gossip will be stopped in its tracks. Such self-control is possible in the Spirit-filled life.

> *Breathe on me, breath of God,*
> *Until my heart is pure,*
> *Until with Thee I will one will,*
> *To do and to endure.*
>
> —"Breathe on Me, Breath of God"
> Edwin Hatch
> *Sing to the Lord* 302
> *Worship in Song* 303

* * *

Father, how easy it is to allow our words and deeds to go unchecked. What damage is done, what sorrow is caused, when we fail to live disciplined lives. I borrow today a Psalmist's prayer: "May the words of my mouth and the meditation of my heart be pleasing in your sight, O Lord, my Rock and my Redeemer." Amen!

23. The Spirit-filled Life: Attainments

I do not count myself to have apprehended; but one thing I do, forgetting those things which are behind and reaching forward to those things which are ahead, I press toward the goal for the prize of the upward call of God in Christ Jesus (Phil. 3:13-14, NKJV).

Too many Christians assume that since they have been filled with the Spirit they have reached their goal. This is far from the truth. Being filled with the Spirit equips us for growth and spiritual attainments. Progress is the law of both physical and spiritual growth. Self-complacency is always a mark of decline. May we never be satisfied with the initial experience of being filled with the Spirit. There is much ground ahead to be possessed.

It is true that purity is an instant work of grace, but maturity is a process. It is right to be satisfied with what we have but never with what we are. God is not through with us yet. Our sincere prayer and aim is higher ground.

> *I'm pressing on the upward way;*
> *New heights I'm gaining ev'ry day,*
> *Still praying as I onward bound,*
> *"Lord, plant my feet on higher ground."*
>
> —"Higher Ground"
> Johnson Oatman, Jr.
> *Sing to the Lord* 467
> *Worship in Song* 278

This ambition is save—to be all that we can possibly be for God, His kingdom, and the souls of men.

It is God's command and will that we be filled with the Spirit. Have you been so filled?

Spirit of God, descend upon my heart.
    Wean it from earth; through all its pulses move.
Stoop to my weakness, mighty as Thou art,
    And make me love Thee as I ought to love.

—"Spirit of God, Descend"
George Croly
Sing to the Lord 298
Worship in Song 267

* * *

Almighty Father, I have nothing and can achieve nothing apart from Your grace and power. Enable me and then I will do Your will and work. Your Word declares that You give power to the faint. I qualify for the promise and claim it for today's living. Be the foundation and the force of my life for Your glory. Amen.

24. The Spirit-filled Life: Power

I was with you in weakness, in fear, and in much trembling. And my speech and my preaching were not with persuasive words of human wisdom, but in demonstration of the Spirit and of power, that your faith should not be in the wisdom but in the power of God (1 Cor. 2:3-5, NKJV).

Some have insisted that the Spirit-filled will always have a sense of power. Though Paul said he experienced "weakness, . . . fear, and . . . much trembling," he did not allow these conditions to keep him from doing what God had called him to do. He was in an area where Greek orators excelled in speaking with persuasive words. But Paul did not want the Corinthians to base their faith on his human skill but on the power of the Holy Spirit. Human weakness is an opportunity for the display of divine power as we depend wholly on God.

A constant sense of power could be dangerous, for it could generate a spirit of self-sufficiency and pride. The wire that carries electricity gives no outward sign of the power it carries, but it is there all the same. It is our responsibility to see that we are well and truly linked up to God, who is the source of power, so that the power of the Spirit will flow through the wire of our lives to His glory.

Frail children of dust, and feeble as frail,
In Thee do we trust, nor find Thee to fail.
Thy mercies how tender, how firm to the end!
Our Maker, Defender, Redeemer, and Friend!

—"O Worship the King"
Robert Grant
Sing to the Lord 64
Worship in Song 6

* * *

My Father, apart from You I can do nothing. Help me to keep the connection with You unbroken, that Your power may ceaselessly flow to me and through me. My responsibilities would daunt me if I had to rely on my own resources alone. Instead, I acknowledge my weakness and appropriate Your power by faith. Amen.

25. The Spirit-filled Life: Success

Now about spiritual gifts, brothers, I do not want you to be ignorant.... There are different kinds of gifts, but the same Spirit. There are different kinds of service, but the same Lord. There are different kinds of working, but the same God works all of them in all men (1 Cor. 12:1, 4-6).

Paul catalogues at least nine specific gifts—all by the same Spirit. Does being Spirit-filled mean that I will be outstandingly successful? It is true that some men and women, after being filled with the Spirit, became remarkably successful in the work of the Lord. If success means great publicity and popularity in religious circles, the devil will work on it to appeal to pride and self-glory. But the essential fact for all is that God fills us with His Spirit in order that we may effectively do His will. Success is incidental and not to be sought after. The vast majority of Spirit-filled Christians will probably remain unknown and unnoticed as they go about quietly doing God's will.

There are two facts to remember. First, there are great variations in the gifts or abilities God has given us. Our capacities vary as does a bucket from a thimble, but each of us may be filled to capacity.

Second, we must remember that there is a difference between the gifts of the Spirit and the gift of the Spirit. The gift of the Spirit is for all, while the gifts of the Spirit vary according to individuals. Doing the will of God at all times is the evidence of a Spirit-filled life. Success, as men rate success, is incidental to this.

All for Jesus! all for Jesus!
  All my being's ransomed pow'rs:
All my tho'ts and words and doings,
  All my days and all my hours.

—"All for Jesus"
Mary D. James
Sing to the Lord 470
Worship in Song 291

* * *

Gracious Father, I am not in competition with Your other children. I assume responsibility for the use of my gifts, but I also rejoice in their gifts. By using those gifts they enrich my life. In some way, however modest, make me helpful to them. Dismiss from my thinking the world's notion of success. Unless I do Your will I am a failure, whatever I may achieve or possess. I pray not to be successful but to be faithful. Amen.

Nina G. Gunter

26. And Then Some

. . . what are you doing more than others? **(Matt. 5:47).**

"Don't promise more than you can do, but do more than you are asked," I heard someone say. The challenge is to be and to do my very best, to be committed to striving for excellence. The apostle Paul stated it well: "Not as though I had already attained, . . . but I follow after" (Phil. 3:12, KJV).

Carl Holmes tells of a retired business executive who was asked the secret of his triumphs. He summed it up in three words: "and then some."

The executive said he discovered at an early age that most of the difference between average people and the achievers could be explained in these words. The achievers did what was expected of them—and then some. They were considerate, kind, and helpful—and then some. They could be counted on—and then some.

Jesus gave us an example of such service. He fed the 5,000 men, plus women and children—and then some. He gave such adequate assistance to Peter and his fishing buddies that the nets were full—and then some. He gives us needed grace—and then some. He enables us to be conquerors—and then some.

I accept the challenges of God through the Church, not as sheer duty and not as drudgery. Within myself I am committed to live at full potential—and then some. Will you join me on this journey?

Give of your best to the Master;
Give Him first place in your heart.
Give Him first place in your service;
Consecrate ev'ry part.

—"Give of Your Best to the Master"
Howard B. Grose
Sing to the Lord 540
Worship in Song 340

*   *   *

Father, You are worthy of the best I can do, and then some. You are worthy of my deepest love and highest praise, and then some. For your glory I want to live by Jesus' "doctrine of the extra." Help me to do so, in His name. Amen.

27. Consumer or Producer?

Serve one another in love **(Gal. 5:13).**

"This is the day of the consumer. Satisfy the customer. He is king." A businessman shared these revealing words with me.

They reflect the consumer mentality of our day. The Church must reject this philosophy. As Christians, we are called away from the values and life-styles of the worldlings who cry, "Satisfy me. Fulfill me. Entertain me. Do it my way. What more can my church do for me?"

God's family is to be one great body of servants. Our Lord himself, as Head of the body, set before us the example of lowly service. "God so loved the world that he gave . . ." "The Son of Man did not come to be served, but to serve . . ." Our Lord laid down His life for others. He was obedient even unto death. *Remind us, O God, that we are never more like You than when we serve.*

The servant mentality is reflected in the person who sincerely asks God, "How can I best serve my church?" "What is my place of ministry?" "What would You have me to be . . . to do . . . to say . . . to give?" God's servant is God's person in God's place doing God's work in God's way. May your leadership and mine reflect the heart of a servant . . . a giver . . . a producer.

Let us pray as did Ignatius of Loyola: "Teach us, good Lord, to serve thee as thou deservest, to give and not to count the cost, to fight and not to heed the wounds, to toil and not to seek for rest, to labor and not ask for any reward, save that of knowing that we do thy will. Amen."

Ready to go, ready to stay;
Ready my place to fill;
Ready for service, lowly or great;
Ready to do His will.

—"Ready"
A. C. Palmer
Sing to the Lord 553
Worship in Song 343

* * *

Father, You sent Your Son into the world as a servant of human needs. I am His follower, and I can be like Him only as I live for others. The world would allure me with false ideas of self-esteem and success. Keep me true to His example for His sake and glory. Amen.

28. Encourage One Another

Encourage one another (1 Thess. 5:11).

This text was the theme of a workshop for furloughing missionaries. The theme provided a biblical and meaningful framework around which the whole program was designed.

Bruce Larson, in his book *Wind and Fire*, alludes to this thought in pointing out some interesting facts about sandhill cranes:

> It seems these large birds, who commute great distances and traverse continents, have three remarkable qualities. First of all, they rotate leadership. No one bird stays out in front all the time. Second, they choose a leader who can handle turbulence. And then, all during the time one bird is leading, the rest are honking, signaling their affirmation. That's not a bad model for the church. Certainly we need leaders who welcome turbulence and who are aware that leadership ought to be rotated. But most of all, we need a church where we are all honking encouragement.[*]

"Encourage one another"!

> *We share our mutual woes,*
> *Our mutual burdens bear;*
> *And often for each other flows*
> *The sympathizing tear.*
>
> —"Blest Be the Tie That Binds"
> John Fawcett
> *Sing to the Lord* 677
> *Worship in Song* 307

---

[*]Bruce Larson, *Wind and Fire* (Waco, Tex.: Word Books, 1984), 64.

* * *

Our Father, not all can do the same work in Your kingdom and in Christ's church. All of us, though, can encourage one another in the work that each does. Help me to remember that I can accomplish more by encouraging others than I can by working alone. May I give to them the encouragement I would like to receive for myself. Amen.

29. Don't Downplay Discipleship

It is enough for a disciple that he be like his teacher, and a servant like his master (Matt. 10:25, NKJV).

In his book *The Frog in the Kettle*, George Barna warns the Church to be aware of "glaring weakness" in the areas of discipleship and accountability. We must not, as individuals or as a Church, position Christianity as a religion to serve *me* first. We dare not downplay the importance of commitment and obedience.

Christianity is a life-style with a purpose. Theology involves action. Therefore, we take the Great Commission seriously: "Go . . . and teach all nations" (Matt. 28:19, KJV). We cannot merely be African Christians, Asian Christians, Caribbean Christians, American Christians, etc. The Great Commission calls us to be world Christians. A sense of global mission must be woven into the fabric of our being.

The Church is a window of opportunity, not only to commend discipleship, but also to nurture believers in the practice of Christlike living.

More about Jesus let me learn,
More of His holy will discern.
Spirit of God, my Teacher be,
Showing the things of Christ to me.

—"More About Jesus"
Eliza E. Hewitt
Sing to the Lord 498
Worship in Song 122

* * *

Holy Father, I am taught by the Lord Jesus Christ to be and to do. He gives, not ideas to keep in mind, but ideals to express in life. He does not simply inform me, but He inspires and requires action from me. That I may do more for Him, I pray that I may be made more like Him. Amen.

30. What Is Your Mission?

For what is our hope, our joy, or the crown in which we will glory in the presence of our Lord Jesus when he comes? Is it not you? (**1 Thess. 2:19**).

A conductor in the Chicago area was retiring after 40 years of railroad work. At his retirement party he said, "It seems as if I've spent all my life trying to help people get home . . . and I've enjoyed every minute of it."

What a mission—to help people get home! You and I have the happy privilege of helping others make it home to heaven. Involvement in this mission brings joy and a sense of fulfillment. Let's keep at it—"help people get home."

> *Brightly beams our Father's mercy*
> *From His lighthouse evermore;*
> *But to us He gives the keeping*
> *Of the lights along the shore.*
>> —"Let the Lower Lights Be Burning"
>> Philip P. Bliss
>> *Sing to the Lord* 706
>> *Worship in Song* 325

* * *

Father, the home that awaits me in heaven is more real than any place I've lived on earth. I am not chasing a mirage; I am in pursuit of reality. All that afflicts me here will be absent there. All that has value here will be enhanced there. That home is too good not to share! Help me help others reach it. Amen.

31. All of Me There Is to Have

I urge you, brothers, in view of God's mercy, to offer your bodies as living sacrifices ... to God (Rom. 12:1).

Nearly all commentaries tell us that "bodies" is a part used for the whole. We are urged to give all we are and have to God in service.

General William Booth, founder of the Salvation Army, was interviewed in the latter years of his life. He was asked the secret to his tremendous life-changing ministry in the slums of London, the brothel streets of Paris, the opium districts of Hong Kong. Booth thought for a moment, and then through tears he told the interviewer, "The secret of my life and ministry is that God has had all of me there is to have."

O we never can know What the Lord will bestow
Of the blessings for which we have prayed
Till our body and soul He doth fully control,
And our all on the altar is laid.

—"Is Your All on the Altar?"
Elisha A. Hoffman
Sing to the Lord 525
Worship in Song 280

* * *

Father, You held nothing back from us. You gave Your best, Your all, Your only Son! In that same way I would give myself to You. All that I am and have is Yours. Take me and what is mine and use it all for Your glory. I make this living sacrifice, without reservation, in Jesus' name. Amen.

32. Be Still

Be still before the Lord and wait patiently for him (Ps. 37:7).

What a timely admonition! Many things disturb holy stillness. The world is restless. The economy is uncertain. The hearts of people are troubled. The air is filled with noises.

There was a time when the people of God were called "the 'quiet' in the land." That was over 1,900 years ago! But God admonishes us who are so feverishly occupied with external things, "Be still before the Lord." He longs to give us the eternal joy that comes through stillness. He who dwells in eternal stillness says to all restless, exhausted Christians, "Be still. What you need is stillness."

Resolve to seek stillness. Seek the secret place of prayer. Seek to enter that place more often than you have in the past. And then remain in the secret place of prayer until you become still before the Lord.

In stillness you hear eternity. You hear God's message. You receive strength for the tests and assignments of daily Christian living. "Be still before the Lord."

Be still my soul; thy God doth undertake
  To guide the future as He has the past.
Thy hope, thy confidence let nothing shake;
  All now mysterious shall be bright at last.
Be still my soul; the waves and winds still know
His voice who ruled them while He dwelt below.

—"Be Still, My Soul"
Katharina von Schlegel
Sing to the Lord 97
Worship in Song 41

* * *

Father, help me to be hushed before You, that I may not miss Your words to me. I seek in reverent stillness Your grace and guidance for life today in this clamorous world. You are the God of peace. Grant me an inward calm that the pounding seas of fortune and misfortune cannot destroy. From that center of strength I can live triumphantly. Amen.

33. Show and Tell

We will tell the next generation the praisewor-
thy deeds of the Lord **(Ps. 78:4).**

An executive of International Business Machines
boastfully said, "Every employee of IBM, executive or
custodial, knows who Tom Watson is—the founder of
IBM." He proceeded to inform his listeners that this
tradition of passing on information about the heritage
and commitment of IBM was very important to the
ongoing effectiveness and appreciation of the com-
pany. When asked what motivated this tradition, the
executive replied, "The Bible."

God's Word challenges each generation to model
before the next generation the words and works of
God, that each successive generation might "put their
trust in God" (Ps. 78:7).

Will the next generation of Nazarenes embrace
the holiness message and mission that formed the in-
spiring vision of their fathers and mothers? They will
if they see commitment to holiness and mission lived
out in the present generation. But what is not seen in
one generation will not be believed in the next generation. "We will not hide them from their children"
(Ps. 78:4).

O give us homes where Christ is Lord and Master,
    The Bible read, the precious hymns still sung;
Where pray'r comes first in peace or in disaster,
    And praise is natural speech to ev'ry tongue;

Where mountains move before a faith that's vaster,
*And Christ sufficient is for old and young.**

—"A Christian Home"
Barbara B. Hart
Sing to the Lord 727
Worship in Song 499

* * *

Our Father, teach us to teach our children who You are and what You do, that they may experience the wonders of Your saving grace in their own lives. Secondhand religion has no life or power or blessing. They must hear of You and trust in You themselves. Let our God not be a stranger to them. Amen.

*Words copyright © 1965 Singspiration Music/ASCAP. All rights reserved. Used by permission of Benson Music Group.

34. Get What God Can Do

After they prayed, . . . they were all filled with the Holy Spirit and spoke the word of God boldly (Acts 4:31).

Dr. Robert G. Lee said, "If you educate, you get what education can do. And that's good. If you organize, you get what organization can do. And that's good. When you pray, you get what God can do. And that's best."

Why is there a shortage of funds? Why is there a shortage of workers to gather the harvest? There is only one real reason—we have not prayed enough. We "have not, because [we] ask not" (James 4:2, KJV). Prayer is the key to effective global evangelism.

Let us not use the excuse that we do not have time to pray. On the average, a person in the United States watches more than six hours of television daily. Can we not "forsake" some things and be with the Father more? He who waits on God does not lose time. Pray, and "get what God can do."

> *Sweet hour of prayer, sweet hour of prayer,*
> *That calls me from a world of care*
> *And bids me at my Father's throne*
> *Make all my wants and wishes known!*
> *In seasons of distress and grief*
> *My soul has often found relief,*
> *And oft escaped the tempter's snare*
> *By thy return, sweet hour of prayer.*
>
> —"Sweet Hour of Prayer"
> William W. Walford
> *Sing to the Lord* 632
> *Worship in Song* 475

* * *

Faithful Father, You have promised help in time of need for those who come to Your throne of grace in confidence. Trusting Your promise and power I come today. You know my needs and I know Your love. There my soul rests. Amen.

35. God Heals Broken Hearts

He heals the brokenhearted (Ps. 147:3).

A little girl sat attentively in church one Sunday morning. She heard the pastor announce a healing service for that evening. She hurried home, greatly excited, and picked up the worn and ragged baby doll she played with most often. She loved that doll more than all her other dolls, but the week before she had dropped it. Its head fell off and was crushed. Now, she thought, I'll take it to the healing service tonight.

When service time came, and the pastor invited those who wanted to pray for healing to come to the altar, she went forward, clutching her broken doll. She presented it to the pastor, who said gently, "Honey, God doesn't heal baby dolls." Through tears of disappointment she responded, "But, Pastor, God does heal broken hearts."

Whatever breaks our hearts and wrecks our lives is His concern. By prayer and faith, place yourself in His healing hands. Remember, "The Lord delights in those who fear him, who put their hope in his unfailing love" (Ps. 147:11).

Does Jesus care when my heart is pained
Too deeply for mirth and song,
As the burdens press, And cares distress,
And the way grows weary and long?
O, yes, He cares; I know He cares!
His heart is touched with my grief.
When the days are weary, The long nights dreary,
I know my Savior cares.

—"Does Jesus Care?"
Frank E. Graeff
Sing to the Lord 574
Worship in Song 456

* * *

Compassionate Father, Your heart is pained when my heart is broken. Your Word assures me that in all my afflictions You are afflicted. I cannot fathom such love, but I depend upon it. Bring the healing of Your love to my heart, and in its strength I will serve the brokenhearted around me. Amen.

36. One Plus One Does Not Equal Two

For we are God's fellow workers (1 Cor. 3:9).

A log-pulling contest was held in the Northwest to see how many pounds each horse could pull. The winning horse pulled about 10,000 pounds. The second-place horse pulled about 9,700 pounds.

Then the people decided to put the two horses together to see how much they could pull. Most thought it would be about 20,000 pounds, but together the horses pulled 50,000 pounds.

One plus one does not always equal two. We can accomplish more as a team than the sum of our labors as individuals. Working together with God greatly multiplies our effectiveness.

Casey Stengel, legendary manager of the New York Yankees baseball team, once said, "It's easy to get good players. Getting them to play together, that's the hard part." For the Kingdom's sake, let's pull together!

> *In Him shall true hearts ev'rywhere*
> *Their high communion find;*
> *His service is the golden cord*
> *Close binding all mankind.*
>
> —"In Christ There Is No East or West"
> John Oxenham
> *Sing to the Lord* 678
> *Worship in Song* 306

* * *

O Father, "from whom [Your] whole family in heaven and on earth derives its name," help me to be a cheerful and cooperative worker with others who seek to make known Your Son, our Savior, Jesus Christ. Amen.

37. Holding the Ropes

Then the disciples took [Saul] by night, and let him down by the wall in a basket (Acts 9:5, KJV).

Praying for missions has been likened to holding the ropes for missionaries and other workers at the front line.

John Wesley said, "God does nothing but by prayer, and everything with it." Samuel Chadwick stated, "Satan dreads nothing but prayer. His one concern is to keep the saints from praying." Jesus said, "Ask, and you will receive, that your joy may be full" (John 16:24, NKJV).

The world mission movement was born in prayer, and it will only survive by prayer. Prayer is the ignition to global evangelism. Prayer is the lifeblood of missions. We will never reach a lost world for Christ with glitzy performances, religious one-liners, and slick packaging. The clarion call is for Christians who will commit themselves to serve as intercessors.

Holding the ropes lifts God's missionaries over the walls—the walls of despair, loneliness, financial difficulties, indifference, and barrenness. Prayer enables you to extend your ministry throughout the world. It gives you entrée anywhere in the world. By prayer you can accompany missionaries to remote reaches of the earth, and be a partner in their healing, teaching, and evangelizing ministries. God help us to pray!

Let us pray that grace may ev'rywhere abound:
    "Send the light! Send the light!"
And a Christlike spirit ev'rywhere be found.
    Send the light! Send the light!

—"Send the Light"
Charles H. Gabriel
Sing to the Lord 705
Worship in Song 351

* * *

Father, I commit myself to intercede for those who have committed themselves to proclaim the gospel to distant places and peoples. Let me share in their labors that I may rejoice also in their victories. Holding the ropes is so important! Make my hands strong and I will not complain of blisters. Amen.

38. We Don't Count the Cost!

I consider everything a loss compared to the surpassing greatness of knowing Christ Jesus my Lord, for whose sake I have lost all things (Phil. 3:8).

On a tour through a cathedral in Mexico, a man noticed a golden statue. He said to the Mexican tour guide, "The golden statue is dazzlingly beautiful! What did it cost?"

With a quizzical look on her face the tour guide replied, "Cost? When it's for our God we don't count the cost."

Oh, that more Christians felt toward their Lord as did that Mexican tour guide, and deemed no sacrifice too dear so that the gospel might be sent to the ends of the earth!

Jesus said, "No one . . . can be My disciple who does not give up all his own possessions" (Luke 14:33, NASB).

> *Take my lips, and let them be*
> *Filled with messages for Thee.*
> *Take my silver and my gold—*
> *Not a mite would I withhold.*
>
> —"Take My Life, and Let It Be Consecrated"
> Frances R. Havergal
> *Sing to the Lord* 455
> *Worship in Song* 281

* * *

Father, the precious blood of Christ was invested for our salvation. In the light of Calvary, I cannot give less than my all to make Your saving love known to others. Help me to withhold nothing from You. In my giving and living I want to reflect Yours. Amen.

39. Choose One Chair

Choose for yourselves this day whom you will serve, ... But as for me and my household, we will serve the Lord (Josh. 24:15).

The *Alliance Life* magazine in 1991 carried a meaningful article about Luciano Pavarotti, the peerless tenor in the opera world. Pavarotti trained for years with a professional tenor in his hometown of Modena, Italy, and at the same time he attended a teacher's college. Pavarotti came to the crossroads for making his life-long commitment. He asked his father, "Shall I be a teacher or a singer?" His father wisely replied, "Luciano, if you try to sit on two chairs you will fall between them. For life, you must choose one chair."

We must choose one chair. Jesus said, "No man can serve two masters." Let us serve Jesus Christ with a single-hearted devotion. For many, doing this will mean increased involvement in the kingdom of God. Sit in one chair!

> *All to Jesus I surrender;*
> *All to Him I freely give.*
> *I will ever love and trust Him,*
> *In His presence daily live.*

> —"I Surrender All"
> Judson W. Van Deventer
> *Sing to the Lord* 486
> *Worship in Song* 287

* * *

Father, I pray as did the ancient Psalmist, "Give me an undivided heart, that I may fear your name. I will praise you, O Lord my God, with all my heart; For great is your love toward me." Don't let me be torn between You and anyone or anything else. Fix my heart forever upon yourself, where it belongs. Amen.

40. Are You There?

Then the word of the Lord came to him: "Go at once to Zarephath of Sidon and stay there. I have commanded a widow in that place to supply you with food" **(1 Kings 17:8-9).**

A television interviewer said to Bob Cousey, great basketball player, "Many of your fans are asking why you don't look at your teammate when you pass the ball to him."

Bob quickly replied, "I never pass [the ball] to where my teammate is. I pass it to where he ought to be!"

Unless we are where God wants us to be, we will not maximize His power or plan for our lives.

Elijah would have missed the ravens who brought him food had he not been at the brook Cherith. The Lord said, "I have ordered the ravens to feed you there" (1 Kings 17:4). Had he gone from there to any place but Zarephath he might have starved, for a widow there had been commanded to feed him.

Where God wills, there He works. Be sure you are "there"—centered in His will.

Anywhere with Jesus I can safely go,
Anywhere He leads me in this world below.
Anywhere without Him dearest joys would fade.
Anywhere with Jesus I am not afraid.

—"Anywhere with Jesus"
Jessie B. Pounds
Sing to the Lord 614
Worship in Song 330

* * *

Father, the only place on earth where I can be secure, useful, and happy is the place of Your choice for me. No measure of comfort or pleasure could compensate the loss I would suffer if I were out of Your will. Name the place and I shall say yes. There I will go and there You will be. In Your presence I will find my peace. Amen.